Fa...... s
Volume Two

NHS
Ambulances
The First
25 Years
1948 - 1973

by

Chris Batten

NOSTALGIA ROAD

CONTENTS

Front Cover: *A preserved Austin Princess, UWV 753 that was formerly with the Wiltshire Ambulance Service.*

Rear Cover Top: *A Ford Transit ambulance demonstrator GOO 14N with diesel engine and Lomas body on test in the West Midlands. Ford of Great Britain*

Rear Cover Bottom: *Two Dennis Karrier ambulances employed by Surrey Ambulance Service, with registration numbers MPH 888D and MPH 967D.*

Left: *A January 1952 view of a Bedford K1 working in the North Yorkshire Moors, where it is pictured descending a 1 in 3 farm track. Vauxhall Motors Ltd.*

Right: *A line up of six Bedford J1 ambulances serving with Bradford City Council in 1961. Vauxhall Motors Ltd.*

ISBN 0-9521070-3-1
2nd imprint - August 1998
British Cataloguing in Publication Data
A catalogue record for this book is available from the British Library

The **Nostalgia Road**™ Series
is conceived, designed and produced
by

Trans Pennine Publishing Ltd.

PO Box 10
Appleby-in-Westmorland
Cumbria, CA16 6FA
Tel. 017683 51053
Fax. 017683 53558
e-mail trans.pennine@virgin.net

Reprographics by
Barnabus Design & Repro
Threemilestone, Truro
Cornwall, TR4 9AN
01872 241185

And Printed in Cumbria by
Howe of Brampton Ltd.,
Townfoot Industrial Estate,
Brampton, Cumbria CA8 1SW
016977 2447

Trans-Pennine and Howe of Brampton are both **Quality Guild** registered companies.

© *Trans-Pennine Publishing 1998,* TEXT: *Chris Batten ,* PHOTOGRAPHS: *British Ambulance Society or As Credited*

INTRODUCTION

This book traces the development of the British ambulance following the introduction of the provisions of the National Health Act 1946, which became effective from 5th July 1948. This placed, for the first time, a responsibility on local authorities to provide a comprehensive ambulance service in their area. Before the passing of the Act there were a variety of arrangements that existed in county districts; some operated ambulances from fire or police stations, some from Council yards, others from local garages, whilst several relied upon various agency or local volunteer agreements.

This volume concentrates on the first 25 years of the national ambulance service and covers the problems faced by local authorities in the early post-war years when taking over the previous 'ad-hoc' arrangements. It discusses the shortages of new vehicles and lack of trained staff, then recalls the golden age of the 1950s and 1960s, with such classic ambulances as the Daimler DC27. In conclusion it brings the reader to the early 1970s with the coming of more standardisation when authorities began utilising commercial van chassis such as the ubiquitous Ford Transit and the Bedford CF.

The early 1970s is really a good place to break the story, for as we will see, prior to local government reorganisation, the services and ambulances operated by the different authorities varied considerably. The second 25 years covers the period when the NHS ambulance service was more consolidated, because following reorganisation in 1974 the approach to operations was far more unified, but that is another story. At the outset it is appropriate to mention the valuable contribution made to this book by the **British Ambulance Society**, which is rapidly becoming recognised for the role it is playing in recording and preserving our ambulance history and heritage. Many of the photos in this book have been obtained from Society archives and thanks are hereby recorded for the assistance given. (Unless credited otherwise, all the images used are supplied by kind permission of the Society.) Where known, acknowledgement has been given to the original donor or source, but if anyone has been missed this is unintentional and thanks are given to all of those who have assisted the aims of the Society. Acknowledgement and thanks are especially due to Roger Leonard for his valuable assistance and use of photos from his own collection.

Chris Batten, Tonbridge, Kent, 5th July 1998.

THE POSITION POST-WAR

Because of lack of resources, many ambulance service organisers continued using wartime utilitarian conversions after the war. The Home Ambulance Service (a joint St. John Ambulance/British Red Cross Society organisation) supplemented local services and had over 1,000 ambulances available stationed throughout the British Isles.

The operation of these vehicles, when required, was undertaken mainly by voluntary workers. To build up their fleet in 1945/46, a large-scale conversion of ex-military ambulances was undertaken. It was mainly Austin K2s that were inspected, but only those in good condition and with less than 40,000 miles (64,370 Kms) on the clock were accepted for conversion. The Home Ambulance Service's own repair workshops at Lots Road, Chelsea, carried out most of the chassis renovation, whilst bodywork conversions were undertaken by a number of coachwork companies. Other vehicles in the fleet were based on Austin and Bedford vehicles. The livery of the Home Ambulance Service at this period was dark blue with black wings.

Top:
An Austin ambulance operated by Lindsey County Council with a utilitarian body built by Lomas. Note the deflectors on the headlights, which are a legacy of wartime blackout regulations. This typifies the sort of vehicle providing ambulance cover in the immediate post-war years. The Lindsey service had an ivory livery from 1948, but after it was divorced from the fire service in 1963, the Chief Officer George Turner introduced a pretty powder blue scheme in 1964.
Photo: British Ambulance Society courtesy R.Henderson
Centre:
This 1925 Austin 20hp Ambulance, fitted with an old horse-ambulance body by Wilson & Stockall, passed to Lancashire County Council in 1948 and by then it was looking every bit it's age.
Photo: British Ambulance Society Archives courtesy Lancashire County Ambulance Service
Bottom:
A Bedford K type ambulance of The Home Ambulance Service, in London in 1948. This vehicle has a 'Premier' body built by Pilchers of Wimbledon, and contained Carter's Minor Low Loading Stretcher Gear, with provision for either a second stretcher or bench seating. To further ease loading there was a full-width rear step.
Top Right:
An American Trailer Ambulance Unit on a Ford V8 Chassis, as supplied to Lancashire Constabulary and used in the Furness area. This is an American designed Model 78, with a 3622cc side-valve engine, but built in Britain between 1937 and June 1938.
Photo courtesy: Lancashire County Constabulary

THE EARLY YEARS

With the passing of the National Health Act 1946, all local authorities had to introduce a comprehensive ambulance service by the implementation date of 5th July 1948. Most principal cities and towns in Britain had long been running well-organised services, but many remote areas had been largely dependent upon voluntary organisations such as the St. John Ambulance, or services run on an agency basis. A great amount of work was thus necessary to obtain vehicles, depots and staff coupled with the requirement to ensure an operational system that could provide ambulance cover at all hours. The problems of this period cannot be over-emphasised. Firstly there was a chronic shortage of new vehicles, with those made available from previous operators mainly past their best, whilst even the youngest had served through the difficulties of the war years. The quality and training of staff was another area where standards varied greatly. How the new service was organised was left up to each County authority, but there were real practical problems.

Left:
A trio of ambulances handed over to Lancashire County Council on the inception of the National Health Service in 1948. From the left, the vehicles pictured are a 1938 Ford V8 (Model 68) with a wartime body, a Talbot and an Austin.
Photo: British Ambulance Society Archives courtesy Lancashire County Ambulance Service

Below:
An American Trailer Ambulance Unit presented to the people of Lancashire by Mrs. Reynolds Albertini. These vehicles were multi-functional, and could be used to provide both an emergency field kitchen and traditional ambulance duties. Although it may look like a mere 'tea van' CRO 501 could be easily converted to fulfill an emergency role. It is pictured at Ulverston when new in 1942 or 1943.
Photo: Lancashire County Constabulary

The subject was considered in 1950 by a Special Report of the County Medical Officer of Health on the *Operation of the Ambulance Service in the Administrative County of Lancashire* and covered the period 5th July 1948 to 31st March 1950. Before the Act, Lancashire had 109 separate districts in which there was a wide variety of arrangements for the provision of ambulance services; but the new authority found that there was too little nucleus to provide the basis for the services expected after the Act was introduced. Indeed, of the 126 ambulances inherited on 5th July 1948, 74 were more than 10 years old and nine more were over 20 years old.

Left
This is a representative view of ambulance provision in the Red Rose county in the early days of the NHS. Here we see a Lancashire County Council Ambulance Station in Manchester with three Commer/Karrier's and a Hillman Minx sitting-case vehicle.

Bottom:
This 'pool' ambulance registered number ETE 408 is a 1939 Bedford 28, which was reconditioned in November 1948 to assist with the shortage of vehicles. This served with Lancashire County Council until sufficient post-war ambulances became available.

Apart from the shortage of vehicles, and the catchment areas for hospitals not matching local authority boundaries, there were uncertainties over funding as well. The result was a widely contrasting response from the authorities. Some set up their own independent new ambulance services, such as Lancashire, whilst others like Dudley Birmingham and Wolverhampton formed joint 'Fire and Ambulance Services'. A clause in the 1946 Act enabled local authorities to co-operate with the voluntary services of the St. John Ambulance and the British Red Cross Society as well as continuing other local arrangements and these lasted in some areas for a number of years.

Where authorities provided their own service, the ambulances were often regarded as part of the municipal vehicle fleet. In Salford for example, the service came under the transport department and were painted in the same green as Salford City Transport buses; the original 'ambulance' uniforms given to crews were in fact Salford bus inspectors' uniforms. Ambulance crews were normally thought of merely as drivers with the only qualification required being an ability to drive. Generally, only a basic knowledge of first aid training was given to the crews.

This concept lasted for a long time and made it difficult for ambulance personnel to achieve recognition for their profession. To illustrate the problems and the effect the new Act had on ambulance procurement and development, Lancashire County Council is now taken as an example.

Above:
A Morris CV 11 (KTE 35) with Morris Commercial bodywork serving with Lancashire County Council Ambulance Service in 1948.

The supply situation of ambulances presented a serious initial problem, but the St. John Ambulance Brigade rendered valuable help by placing its facilities at Lancashire County Council's disposal. Recognising that the vehicles it had would be inadequate both in numbers and quality, the Health Committee prepared a specification of vehicles to meet their particular needs. Lancashire decided that as most of their ambulance work would be in built-up districts, and over comparatively limited areas, the engines should be of moderate power and thus more economical. Accordingly the County Council invited tenders from 9 distributors (representing the leading manufacturers in the motor trade at the time), for the delivery of 5 ambulances without any restriction as to design or specification. Two firms declined to tender, but of the remainder most quoted delivery dates of between 18-24 months.

The shortage of new vehicles and long deliveries arose because manufacturers were severely restricted in their steel allocation and this was also a time when they were having to meet heavy demands on their production for the export quotas. The 1946 Act also meant that all local authorities were having to obtain ambulances at the same time, which further exasperated the problem. After a period of consideration Lancashire decided to standardise on a single manufacturer and they found that the Rootes Group (Commer/Karrier) appeared to be the only maker who could meet their demands. The Commer/Karrier was thus chosen to become the standard ambulance in Lancashire, and negotiations were held about the supply position.

Eventually an order was placed for 40 ambulances to be delivered in the year ending 31st March 1949, and a similar number were ordered for delivery during the following financial year. The net cost of the standard Commer/Karrier ambulance to the council's specification (including painting in the Lancashire County Ambulance Service colours of cream and maroon) was £1,462 per ambulance. However, it was also found that more specialised vehicles were required for the conveyance of patients over longer distances.

Four vehicles with a chassis long enough to enable the patient to be carried on a stretcher bed within the wheelbase were required, and these had to be powered by a 27hp 6-cylinder engine. Taking into account the need to standardise where possible, the Commer Q3-type ambulance was selected. The cost of these in 1948 including special internal fittings and painting was £1,954 each.

The other need for the new service was the transport of sitting cases, mainly to hospitals for outpatient treatment. It was found that the Hillman Minx Utility met the requirements and 30 of these were ordered in 1948 with a further 30 to follow in 1949. The net cost of these was £585 13s 4d each. Through these acquisitions, by February 1950 Lancashire had a fleet of 216 ambulances to meet their needs, and of this number 147 were reasonably new and standardised on the Rootes Group.

Below:
Lancashire County Council Ambulance Service Commer Q3-type (registered number LTB 674) used for long distance patient transfers. It is amazingly modern-looking when compared with the Austin of 1925, which had been inherited by the service in 1948.

Local authorities throughout Britain experienced similar problems to those described for Lancashire, and to address these difficulties some innovative plans were implemented. For example, Middlesex County Council purchased 62 Morris Commercial heavy fire-pump units, which were designated as surplus to requirement by the Auxiliary Fire Service in October 1947. Of these wartime vehicles, 51 were re-bodied as front-line emergency ambulances, 6 were converted to ambulance coaches and the remainder broken up for use as spares.

The conversions were relatively cheap with new ambulance bodies by J.S. Keen & Company of Hackney, and also Stewart & Arden, each costing about £750 per conversion. The chassis were renovated by a number of firms including Hampshire Car Bodies (HCB) at an average cost of £460 per chassis. So highly thought of were the vehicles produced, that when new chassis did become available, Middlesex County Council provided them with similar bodies, and the type remained in service until 1964. Some of these vehicles were later transferred to the Middlesex County Civil Defence Pool and these remained active up to 1965. The livery of Middlesex County Council was pale cream with black wings and lining. This situation was typical of many authorities in the postwar era, and it was obvious that new vehicles would have to be provided to satisfy the demands imposed by the newly formed NHS. It was a question of whether the manufacturers would respond to the need, particularly in a period of severe austerity and material shortages.

This Middlesex County Council Morris Commercial ambulance seen above at Hayes Fire Station in 1952, demonstrates that many authorities tended to house emergency ambulances at Fire Stations.
Photo: British Ambulance Society Archives courtesy Charles Keevil.

THE BEDFORD 'UTILICON'

The lack of a suitable commercial chassis for ambulance use, together with the new requirement arising from the 1946 National Health Service Act to carry sitting case patients, led to authorities looking at smaller dual purpose vehicles. One of the first types was the Bedford Utilicon, which was based on a well established chassis from this maker. Accordingly, Martin Walter Ltd. of Folkestone announced the Utilicon All-Purpose Ambulance in 1948.

For a price of £478 they would convert the standard PCV light van, to offer accommodation for five sitting patients or one stretcher patient plus an attendant. To ease the loading of stretcher cases, runners were fitted along one side of the floor and a loading ramp was provided. Roof ventilation was incorporated and safety glass used for all windows. No modifications were made to the mechanical side as the Bedford PC chassis, with its independent front-wheel suspension and double-acting shock absorbers, was thought particularly suitable in its standard form for ambulance work.

Interestingly, the seats and stretcher could be quickly folded away to leave a completely flat floor that could be used for carrying medical equipment or stores. A special seat was also provided to allow the attendant to sit beside the stretcher when required.

Top:
A new Bedford Utilicon Ambulance, is seen here on delivery to the Gloucestershire Ambulance Service.

LONDON AMBULANCES

London County Council like everyone else found itself short of ambulances after the war, although they had been providing cover in the capital since 1930 when they took over the services previously provided by the Metropolitan Assylums Board and 25 Boards of Guardians. This service had been bravely continued through the dark days of World War II in conjunction with the London Auxiliary Ambulance Service. At its peak, the wartime service in Greater London included several thousand vehicles and over 10,000 auxiliary ambulance personnel. The ambulances they used ranged from private cars to goods vehicles that were brought into service at night after they had already done their day's commercial duties. There were more than 100 ambulance stations, and some of these (and their staff) suffered heavily from enemy action.

By the end of 1945, some 48,709 war casualties had been assisted by the service. So, by virtue of its experience and the size of fleet, London had more flexibility and the changes of the NHS Act had less impact. However, London also had an eye to the future and was quickly taking initiatives in ambulance design.

An early move was the construction of a 'prototype' ambulance body on a specially lengthened Bedford 30cwt chassis in 1947. The LCC had a large advantage over most other authorities however, in that it had its own superbly equipped workshops at Wandsworth which were capable of producing the new bodies. Here they produced the prototype Bedford, which carried the LCC Fleet number '1131' and originally had the registration number HYF 541.

London ambulances were almost always white, but this prototype was painted in a two-tone livery (the actual colours are not known) with the coloured waistband extending over the bonnet area. There was a single rear door, surprisingly hinged on the nearside, which meant that the crews would have to walk into the road to gain access.

Top and Centre:
A selection of photographs showing London's attempt to resolve the postwar ambulance shortages, with pictures that demonstrate the prototype ambulance 1131. The first picture shows the prototype Bedford , ' in its two-tone livery with the word 'PROTOTYPE' stencilled above the 'AMBULANCE' lettering on the sides, whilst the second view presents the rear aspect.

Bottom:
This later photo appears to show Fleet No. 1131 with registration number JXA 845 and without the darker paintwork, whether this vehicle was a re-registration, re-bodying or duplicate use of the same fleet number is unclear.

AUSTIN K8/AA WELFARER

Another ambulance of the period was the Austin Welfarer, which was a commercial variant of the Austin 3-Way van on a 25cwt chassis. Austin had first promoted the 'Welfarer' at the 1948 Commercial Motor Show at Earls Court, where they 'launched' a special version of the K8 model with an ambulance body built at the Austin works.

Designated the Welfarer K8/AA, it had several modifications to the standard chassis that were intended to meet the special needs of ambulance work. These included smaller wheels (7.50 by 16) and wider tyres, as well as softer road springs and appropriate shock absorber settings to provide a smoother ride for patients. A wide ranging choice of seating and stretcher arrangements were offered including two bench seats that accommodated sitting cases on each side, a single bench seat and stretcher or a double stretcher version.

Heating and ventilation were also given special attention with two drop-down windows of tinted glass on either side as well as thermal and sound insulation fitted along the body walls. In addition the Welfarer was fitted with a Clayton air conditioning system, which drew air through a Vokes filter from a roof-mounted intake. When required this could be heated by the engine coolant water, whilst full air circulation was maintained by an extractor in the roof. The complete price, less stretchers or patient seating, was £805.

The LCC decided to evaluate the Welfarer for the London service who gave the 'test' vehicle fleet number '1500' and licensed it with the very appropriate registration number JXE 999. However, in the end London did not pursue widespread use of the Welfarer and they chose another avenue of approach. Even so, the Welfarer was a popular ambulance in its day and it saw service with a number of counties including Birmingham, Cornwall, Cumberland, Hampshire, Kent, Warwickshire and Worcestershire.

Above:
The evaluation model Austin Welfarer in service with London County Council as Fleet No. '1500'.
Left:
This Kent County Council Austin Welfarer, with the registration KKM 883, was pictured at Sevenoaks in the early 1950s.
Photo: Chris Batten

Top Right:
A Ford 7V ambulance of Essex County Council, with bodywork by Herbert Lomas.
Bottom Right
The interior view of the Ford 7V ambulance showing the dark working area and low headroom that crews had to contend with.
Photos: British Ambulance Society Archives, but both originally promotional photos issued by Ford of Great Britain.

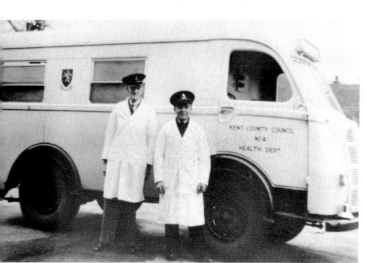

FORD 7V

Despite their later dominant role in the British Ambulance scene, when the Transit became one of the more popular ambulance chassis, it is strange to relate that Ford did not actively pursue this type of business in the post-war years. A few Fords were in use in Britain when the war came to an end, but many of these ambulances were of American origin. Ford's own records show that only a limited number of chassis were 'released' for ambulance building, although from 1948 onwards the Ford Pilot was offered to coach-builders in chassis-cab form as the E71C but there were few takers.

Essex County Council inherited some Ford 7V ambulances in 1948 with bodywork by Herbert Lomas, but this county went on to use Bedfords when they became available. However, the Ford 7V is probably best remembered for its use as the basis for the Triang Minic tinplate model ambulance (which rather strangely had LCC markings). Although Ford were not particularly active in the ambulance market at this time, they were represented at the 1948 Commercial Motor Show by Martin Walter, the coach-builders from Folkestone. They offered the Fordson E83W 10 cwt chassis, which gained some success as a light works/industrial ambulance.

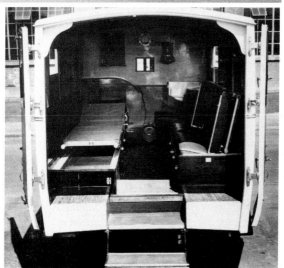

LOCAL AGENCY WORK

An example of a locally provided service operating within the National Health Service was 'The Mile Oak Ambulance' in Staffordshire. An ambulance and the free use of it for the residents of Mile Oak, Fazeley, Drayton Bassett, Canwell and Hints, was initially provided through voluntary subscriptions by local residents, plus many fund-raising events.

After 1948, Staffordshire County Council provided funding for the use of the ambulance in Tamworth and its surrounds. This service ran from its inception in October 1941 until March 1953. By 1951, it was the only voluntary operated ambulance of its kind in the Midlands.

It was even praised by Aneurin Bevan, the then Minister of Health, and was considered good enough to work within the requirements of the National Health Act until Tamworth Ambulance Station was opened by Staffordshire County Council in 1953. The original vehicle was a Ford, which was later replaced with a Humber at a cost of £750.

Above
*The Mile Oak Ambulance was a service operated by volunteers until 1953 and initially used this Ford, but no photo can be traced of the later Humber vehicle that took its place.
Photo: Chris Batten via Tony Brookes of Peel Parishes Papers.*

DAIMLER DC 27

Many people's idea of the post-war ambulance is probably the Daimler Conquest 27hp (DC27), as this stylish vehicle was used as the basis for a Dinky Toys model that was sold for many years. The full size version also achieved great fame and went on to become the classic ambulance of the 1950s.

It came about as a response to the shortage of suitable chassis for ambulance work after the war, when Daimler decided to offer a special ambulance chassis. The ambulance design they finally achieved was a result of collaboration with medical and municipal authorities throughout the country, having sought their views on what would make a good ambulance. Daimler paid special regard for the specific requirements of London County Council, but the contribution that the LCC actually made to the design of the body is not all that well known and should be recorded.

Top Right:
The prototype ambulance body on a 1928 W&G Du Cros modified chassis. Note the tape holding the front assembly to the rear and the folding crew door.
Below:
The prototype ambulance, JXE 466, is pictured under construction at the Wandsworth workshops in July 1947.

Following a feasibility study in 1947, the LCC's Wandsworth workshops constructed a prototype ambulance body which was mounted on the reconstructed chassis and axles of a 1928 W&G Du Cros with a Lincoln Zephyr engine and gearbox. The bodywork had many features that were later used on the production Daimler DC 27s, although it also had items like hinged cab doors and a sloping bottom at the rear, which were not ultimately pursued.

The prototype carried the registration JXE 466 and whilst it never entered operational service, this most interesting vehicle was kept by the LCC for a number of years and it is believed that it may still exist. It appeared at the 1965 Review to celebrate the creation of the Greater London Council (GLC), when the unified London Ambulance Service was formed from parts of nine existing services. This created the largest ambulance service in the world, following the absorption of the ambulance services of London and Middlesex county councils, the boroughs of Croydon, East Ham and West Ham and parts of the Essex, Hertfordshire, Kent and Surrey county council fleets.

Below: *A rear view of the prototype ambulance shows the similarity to the production Daimler DC 27s. The outward sweep at the bottom of the rear panel was not pursued however.*

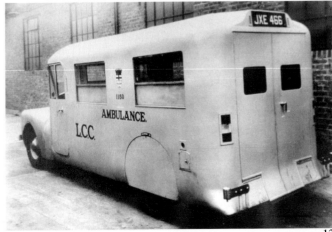

Top:
The classic 1950s ambulance - a Daimler DC 27 of the London County Council Ambulance Service with the registration number KLC 450 and Fleet No. 'A20'.

Centre:
Front and rear views of the London Daimler are represented in this picture of KLC 477 and KLC 545. This interesting picture is very useful as it shows that (at this time) the LCC vehicles had no identification lettering on the rear at all.

Bottom
The last Daimler DC27 to enter service with the LCC - registration number LLA 222 LCC Fleet No. 'A222' and the only Hooper bodied example to serve with London, all the others being Barker bodied. The differences are the single waistline strip and the full length cab doors. It is thought this was a replacement for a written-off vehicle.

The first production Daimler DC 27 appeared in 1949 and was bodied by Barker & Company Coach-builders. They were constructed with an ash framework, and it was found that they offered a smooth and luxurious ride with excellent stability. The only drawbacks were the absence of a door into the cab area from the saloon, which restricted crew access and communications, although a sliding window was provided. Mechanically they suffered high petrol consumption (averaging 8.5 miles per gallon on accident work) and questionable brakes, which resulted in some spectacular accidents.

Unfortunately the cost of this bespoke ambulance was relatively high and sales were not as great as Daimler had hoped, despite extensive promotion. Only 499 were built, with London standardising on the Daimler and having 222 in their fleet. Other users included Belfast, Birmingham, Carmarthenshire, Croydon, Cumberland, Hertfordshire, Isle of Wight, Nottingham, Plymouth, Salford, Surrey and West Hartlepool. Most Daimler DC 27s were bodied by Barker & Co., but a number received Hooper bodies.

The main difference between the two coach builders was that the Barker design had two raised waistbands whereas the Hooper version only had one. The Daimler DC 27 lasted in service until well into the 1960s and a number have been preserved, including the first production example by the London Ambulance Service historic fleet - registration JXP 63 - LCC Fleet number 'A1'.

In Northern Ireland, the ambulance service has just restored a DC 27, which appeared at the Lord Mayor's Garden Party (attended by HRH Prince Charles) a few weeks before this book went to press. This Daimler had lain derelict for many years, having first been used as a caravan when it was withdrawn from active service.

Right:

Not all ambulances were white and a number of authorities employed some very colourful liveries. For example, Sheffield at one time had ambulances painted in a distinctive yellow and black scheme. The base colours for most ambulance services were often cream, white, grey or blue, but many vehicles were given striking coloured waistbands, wings or roofs as a contrast. Other services went for a darker overall colour, such as maroon, navy blue or dark green (as seen here on this bottle green liveried DC 27 of West Hartlepool Corporation). Often the paint was chosen because it was a 'stock item' and was used on other municipal-owned vehicles such as corporation buses, council lorries or even dustbin wagons.

Left:

This picture provides another example of the type of paint schemes applied in the 1950s, as several ambulance services adopted a two-tone approach. Here we see a Hooper bodied version of the Daimler DC 27 serving with Croydon Ambulance Service. The livery of ORK 8 is an attractive two-tone grey. However, the reader may well question the practicality of choosing grey for an emergency vehicle in these days when 'high visibility' requirements are paramount.

Left:

The Daimler DC27's were notorious for problems with their brakes, and it was not unknown for the rescuers to become the victim as they raced on their missions of mercy. We do not have the details of this event, but the end result is a rather spectacular and ignominious fate for the Daimler. On this occasion it is down to the London Fire Service to effect the rescue.

Opposite Page Top:

At the outset of this book, an editorial decision was taken not to feature pictures of ambulances attending incidents if victims and casualties were portrayed, even though this is the very reason for the ambulance function. Accordingly, the Surrey Ambulance Service Daimler DC 27 seen here is at a 'staged' accident, and the 'victim' is a volunteer. The picture is exceptionally useful however, as the view shows the excellent rear access arrangements for crews.
Photos: British Ambulance Society Archives via Charles Keevil.

Centre Left:

The Daimler DC27 seen here was one of 20 ambulances from this maker that were operated by the Northern Ireland Hospitals Authority between 1948 and 1966. Whilst the NHS Ambulance provisions differed in the province, it is worth recalling the Daimlers' active service. They attended many major accidents over the years, and the Northern Ireland Ambulance Service has recorded just a few of the major incidents in which the DC27's were used. These include the Nutt's Corner Air Disaster, the Princess Victoria ferry sinking, the gangway disaster at the Harland & Wolff shipyard and the explosion aboard the SS Rena Del Pacifico. Fleet number 74 was selected for use as the world's first Cardiac Ambulance until it was eventually replaced by a Karrier -Dennis in 1967. The DC27 pictured here dates from 1952, and was one of the last to be purchased. In active service it carried the fleet number 98, but after its working life it was sold off to a member of the public who converted it to a caravan. After many years it was re-acquired by the NIAS, and it has subsequently been restored by a group of retired ambulance service personnel. Despite its smart appearance in the picture left, it still requires some work doing. The roof ambulance sign has still to be restored, and a working bell has to be found, but these form interesting projects for the future.
Photo: North Of Ireland Ambulance Service

DAIMLER AMBULANCE MODEL DC27

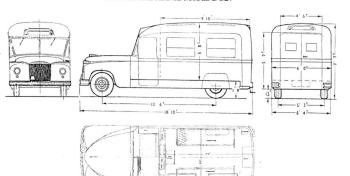

Bottom Left:

A facsimile representation of a scale drawing of a Daimler DC 27 with bodywork by Barker.

THE CHALLENGE OF THE 1950s

The effort put in by Daimler on producing a definitive ambulance, coupled with the demand from the authorities now charged with providing ambulance services, prompted other vehicle manufacturers and bodybuilders to respond to the new market demands. Slowly the immediate post-war shortages were overcome to the extent that when the 1952 Commercial Motor Show was held at Earls Court, much was made of the influence of the Welfare State on ambulance design. A report on the Show records:

'Time was when the ambulance usually subscribed for by the more generous of local inhabitants, carried nothing but stretcher cases and the seriously sick. In days when public transport was much less plentiful, the 'sitting patient' had to make their own way to hospital by tram, bus, train or taxi. However, in 1952, only 10% of ambulance travellers carried by local authorities are stretcher cases and the other 90% are classed as 'sitting cases'. Thus the trend in ambulance building is now towards dual-purpose vehicles. The immediate post-war years saw a heavy demand for the replacement of obsolete fleets which has now largely been satisfied.'

AUSTIN/MORRIS

Morris were well represented at the 1952 Commercial Motor Show by Appleyard of Leeds who were approved ambulance builders to Morris Commercial Cars. They showed a 15-20cwt model that featured low-loading single stretcher gear on the near side and a full-length bench seat on the off-side with upholstered drop arms to give 'sitting case' patients more comfort. This could be removed to enable an extra stretcher to be carried if necessary. They also offered a conversion of the Morris J-type 10cwt van for use in local work. The body was designed to take 6 sitting cases, but three of the seats could also be used to take a single stretcher. Its cost was £735.

Austin also had good representation, and their model 16 taxi chassis was shown by Carbodies who offered it as a model that catered for sitting patients. It followed the general lines of the taxi, but had fully enclosed front seats and large comfortable rear seats with an alternative plan for the provision of a child's stretcher in the rear.

The Austin A125 Sheerline also featured prominently, and this became a popular ambulance in many areas until it was superseded in 1959/60 by the Austin Princess (when the vehicle make became Vanden Plas as this much respected coach-builder became registered as a vehicle manufacturer in their own right). Over the years that followed both models were sold in chassis form to a number of coachbuilders and became very popular with services that could afford the costs of such an ambulance. The firms of Smith/Appleyard and Herbert Lomas built many ambulances on the Sheerline and Princess, both firms for example supplying the City of Birmingham.

Top:
Pictured at the Leeds Road depot of Huddersfield Corporation, this Morris Commercial with an Appleyard body featured a very attractive livery. Its overall body was a pale green, and its roof would have been either grey or a slightly darker shade of green (they varied over the years), whilst the wheel arches and wings were black. The view would date just before the opening of the town's new Ambulance HQ at Marsh.
Photograph: Ian Firth, WYMAS
Centre:
This picture of a Morris Commercial in the Newcastle upon Tyne Ambulance Service was taken on withdrawal in 1963, but it is typical of the Morris units that gave sterling service around the city during the 1950s. To the rear is a Civil Defence Commer Ambulance.
Bottom:
This Austin 16 Taxi chassis has bodywork by Carbodies, and it is pictured in service with the Surrey Ambulance Service. This type of body gave relatively easy access due to its wide doors.

THE AUSTIN A125 AMBULANCE

BODY SPECIFICATION

BODYWORK : *Framing of best quality timber fitted together with heat paint and anti-squeak anti-theft fibres. The exterior panels are of aluminium, the joints being covered by polished mouldings of special alloy. The interior of the ambulance is lined in birch plywood and has polished wood fillets around the windows and waist rail. Special material is coated between the lower and outer casings of the double-skin roof to insulate the interior from heat in summer and cold in winter. The exterior is finished in cellulose, and a choice of colours is available. The interior finish is in cream acid-resisting enamel in withstand fumigation and spraying.*

CAB : *The full-width cab, within will accommodate three persons, is trimmed in hide, while the doors and roof are covered with best quality leathercloth. The wide doors have concealed hinges and enclose the running boards. The partition dividing the cab from the ambulance compartment carries a central sliding window for communication with the attendant. An illuminated "Ambulance" sign is built into the roof above the windscreen.*

WINDOWS : *All windows in the rear compartment are of laminated "Perdid" glass, those in the sides of the body being adjustable and fitted with outside louvres. The rear door glasses are fixed. The fixed windscreen and front door windows are of toughened plate glass.*

VENTILATION AND HEATING : *Ventilation of the body is effected by means of extractor type ventilators on the roof, and to the side windows. A Clayton Dewandre interior heating and air circulating unit is available. The air intake is on the ambulance roof - so far away as possible from fumes and dust - and the heater is thermostatically controlled to ensure an even temperature. Separate heating and air circulation with windscreen demisting is provided for the cab.*

EQUIPMENT : *A selection of equipment is available to suit individual requirements. Provision can be made for two or four stretcher cases or twelve sitting patients, or a combination of stretcher and sitting seats.*

LEADING BODY DIMENSIONS : *Overall length 16 ft. 3½ in. (5.57 m.) ; overall width 6 ft. 5½ in. (1.99 m.) ; overall height (over roof-bar) 7 ft. 7 in. (2.31 m.) ; inside body length in floor level 9 ft. 4 in. (2.54 m.) ; inside body width in waist 5 ft. 4½ in. (1.73 m.) ; inside body height at lowest 5 ft. 1 in. (1.55 m.) ; length of floor from ground 2 ft. 1½ in. (0.65 m.) ; approximate weight (less spare wheel and tools) 47 cwts. (2,387 kgs.).*

* Ambulances for export, other than to Europe, have teak framing.

Above:
The Austin Sheerline Sales Brochure and Specifications.

Above:
An Austin A125 Sheerline owned by Cheshire County Council, who have given it fleet Number 8 and allocated it to Hyde - note that it still has to be registered. The easiest way to differentiate between the two Austin models is that the older Sheerline has large wing-mounted headlamps while the Princess has integral lamps and a much neater front-end appearance.
Photo: R.M Leonard

Above:
This Austin Princess of the Cromer Ambulance Service, Norfolk, was operated jointly by St. John Ambulance and the British Red Cross under an agency agreement which lasted until Norfolk Ambulance Service took over responsibility for the ambulance provision in Cromer. The Princess had a cream and black livery and a bell above the attendants' door.
Photograph: British Ambulance Society via R. Henderson.
Right:
An Austin Princess of West Suffolk County Council with bodywork by Smith/Appleyard, pictured at Newmarket c1967.

THE BEDFORD A & CA TYPES

Other ambulances on display at the 1952 show were the Commer chassis with bodywork by Pilchers and the Bedford 3-ton chassis with bodywork by Spurlings. Such vehicles were to form a significant part of the ambulance market in the UK for the 1950s, but it was noteworthy that Ford had only one ambulance on display and this was for the export market only.

The Bedford A-Type was soon to go on to achieve considerable acclaim, and the versatile chassis saw service in a wide variety of applications. As an ambulance it had bodies by several manufacturers. For example, King's Lynn and Brighton had Lever bodywork, the St. John Ambulance had Spurling, the County of Carnarvonshire used Lomas and the City of Manchester employed Wilson & Stockall.

Bedford also offered a light ambulance for the first time at the 1952 Show, and this was based on the Bedford CA light van chassis. Despite its relatively small size, the CA could carry nine sitting cases or a stretcher and four sitting cases. The firms of Lever, Herbert Lomas and Martin Walter all showed examples of this chassis with the bodywork they were offering. The latter version had a raised roof at the rear so that an attendant could easily stand inside to treat the patient.

Above:
Two A-Type ambulances with Lomas bodies being handed over to Carnarvonshire County Council in 1953. These vehicles both feature a two-tone colour scheme, and the registration numbers are BJC 665 and BJC 666
Photograph: Vauxhall Motors Ltd.

Left:
A Bedford CA with bodywork by Martin Walter of Folkestone for the Croydon Ambulance Service, note the raised rear roof section to assist entry and the forward-facing 'passenger seats' on the vehicles' off-side. The picture of LVB 901 once again reveals the two-tone grey livery of Croydon and the borough crest. As shown here the CA usually had sliding doors for the driver and attendant, but Bedford records show that a few models did have hinged doors.

THE HUMBER PULLMAN

Whilst the Daimler DC 27 was described in the 1952 show report as famous, but lavishly equipped, there was obviously a growing market for other vehicle manufacturers to exploit. We have already seen how Austin did this, and the Humber Motor Company were another manufacturer who tried the concept. Their striking innovation was the Humber Pullman Mk.III ambulance chassis fitted with the Lomas all-metal body. During the 1950s, the Humber chassis went on to become very popular for ambulances and they had a variety of bodies fitted. Among the services using Humber Pullmans and Humber Hawks were Birmingham, Croydon, Nottingham, and the Scottish Ambulance Service, whilst a number were also used by the National Coal Board and Mines Rescue teams.

Top Right:
A Humber Pullman with a Lomas body for the Croydon Ambulance Service (Reg: HRK 686). The Croydon fleet was amalgamated into the London Ambulance Service in the re-organisation of 1965, but by this time the Humber's had all been withdrawn and none were transferred to the London Ambulance Service.

Centre:
A Nottingham City Ambulance Service Humber Pullman finished in a cream livery with Lincoln green lining.

Bottom Right:
Another view of a Croydon ambulance, this time a Humber Hawk with a body by Lomas and the picture is taken from the rear during a staged training incident in the 1950s. The registration number was LOY 400.

Below:
This Scottish Ambulance Service Humber was provided with a two-tone brown livery and had a body by Taggert & Wilson of Motherwell like most Scottish examples.

SCOTLAND

The photograph on page 21 showing a Humber serving with the Scottish Ambulance Service provides an opportunity to explain that the application of the provisions of the 1946 National Health Act were somewhat different north of the border. During World War II, the St. Andrew's Ambulance Association and the British Red Cross Society (Scottish Branch) joined forces under the title 'St. Andrew's and Red Cross Scottish Ambulance Service' with the objective of providing a better means of transport for the sick and injured.

During the period 1946-1948, this joint ambulance service was further developed to meet the needs of all communities in Scotland. So well was this aim carried out, that when the National Health Service Act was introduced, the combined bodies were able to offer the Secretary of State for Scotland an organised, competent and ready-made service to meet the needs of all of Scotland. It was an offer readily accepted.

These six Morris Commercials are awaiting delivery to the Scottish Ambulance Service, and it will be noted that although the vehicles are in the two-tone brown livery they have yet to receive the full markings and lettering.

The existing fleet of the two associations was supplemented by 281 ambulances previously under the control of the Scottish Police authorities, hospitals and industrial bodies especially mines. New ambulances (principally based on the Morris Commercial, Humber and Austin Sheerline chassis) were purchased through the Ministry of Supply with the bodybuilding being put out to tender. The livery was originally two-tone brown, although this was later changed to an attractive blue livery. The joint arrangement with the provision of a national Scottish ambulance service continued until 1967 when the Red Cross withdrew and the service was renamed 'St Andrew's Scottish Ambulance Service'. In 1974 further National Health Service re-organisation saw the ambulance service drop the name 'St. Andrew's' and it became simply 'The Scottish Ambulance Service'.

THE UNUSUAL

There were some unexpected chassis used for ambulance work as these pictures show. For example Herbert Lomas bodied a Bedford TK lorry chassis for use with the City of Gloucester Ambulance Service, and the City of Plymouth Ambulance Service had a Morris 3-ton sitting case ambulance with bodywork by Wadhams Brothers.

Above:
This Bedford TK lorry chassis provided with bodywork by Herbert Lomas, makes for a stylish but unusual new member of the City of Gloucester Ambulance Service. It is pictured prior to being commissioned in service and has yet to be given a number plate.

Right:
Another rare production is this brand new Morris 3-ton for City of Plymouth Ambulance Service with bodywork by Wadhams.

THE NHS ACT IN PRACTICE

The National Health Act 1946 did not specify a common standard of service provision so there were many regional variations, for example by 1953 Cumberland still had no full time administration or operational ambulance staff. The emphasis was on running a service that was as economical as possible. The Cumberland Fleet in 1953 comprised of seven Humber Pullmans, two Daimler DC27's, one Morris Commercial, two Austin Welfarers, and an Austin 2-ton chassis with a Wadhams body. Two new Morris Commercials were ordered with a dual purpose specification to enable either stretcher or sitting case patients to be carried.

Cumberland also endeavoured to minimise the number of personnel required, and wherever possible they used wheeled trolley stretchers so that a single crew member could move a patient. In remote areas agency agreements were maintained with voluntary bodies and the community at large supported 'their' ambulance in a variety of ways. The drivers of these vehicles were usually shopkeepers, post-masters or someone who could easily be contacted by telephone.

Such drivers were paid annual retainers in return for their being willing to turn out whenever required, however in practice this sometimes presented a problem or conflict, especially when the driver was also the retained fire engine driver! Despite this dependence upon part-time helpers, Cumberland claimed that an ambulance could be at any required place in the vastly rural and mountainous county within twenty minutes of an emergency call being received. However, this took no account of the standard of treatment and first aid that would be offered, and typified the view prevalent at the time, that the main role of the ambulance service under the NHS Act was merely to collect patients and transport them to hospital.

By comparison, Birmingham City Council faced very different problems in its predominantly urban territory and before 1948 there were four ambulance providers for the City. The police dealt with all street accidents, the Public Health Department handled infectious cases, tuberculosis sufferers and mental patients, and then there was a voluntary car service run by the British Red Cross, but most ambulance work was carried out by the Birmingham Hospital Contributory Association. This multiplicity of services obviously led to difficulties and the City Council decided to take over direct operational responsibility for an ambulance service in 1948, but entrusted the day-to-day working to the Chief Officer of the City of Birmingham Fire Brigade. By 1953, the Birmingham Fire and Ambulance Service had over 100 ambulances available including a small number for Civil Defence purposes. The fleet included eight Humber Pullmans, six Daimler DC27s, 20 Austin Sheerline's, 20 Austin Welfarer's, 13 Commer's and 10 Morris Commercial's.

In all 262 full-time staff were employed including 10 leading drivers, 158 drivers and attendants, 12 midwives and 13 ambulance cleaners. There was also a Bedford SB Coach that was used to carry expectant mothers for pre-natal treatment at Marston Green Hospital. Thus within 5 years Birmingham had a remarkably efficient and effective ambulance service, which at least attempted to take into account the needs of the patients.

Above:
Birmingham ambulances in their garage showing a Commer and two Austin Welfarer's. The livery of the Birmingham vehicles was cream with a red stripe round the waistline.
Below:
An Austin Sheerline waits in a Birmingham fire station for its next call
Photos: British Ambulance Society Archives via Charles Keevil.

CIVIL DEFENCE

Up until 1965, there was also a standing requirement placed upon local authorities to provide local Civil Defence. Although the work of some elements of this and related services (such as the Green Goddess fire engines) has been well documented, not near so well known is the fact that there was an active Ambulance section of the Civil Defence Corps until this body was finally disbanded in 1968.

The standard Civil Defence ambulance was a very austere vehicle, normally on the Bedford chassis, but they later used Commer and Ford Thames. The early models had no rear doors, and in this they followed the practice adopted for emergency ambulances during the war, when the vehicle was needed to simply 'scoop and run' in order to quickly move as many casualties as an emergency situation might dictate.

Above:
Two Bedford ambulances of the 'County of London Division, Ambulance Section', registration numbers KGK 455 and HXB 508. These vehicles had provision to carry four stretcher patients in a two-up, two-down configuration. There were no doors at the rear of the ambulance, merely a canvas curtain.

The markings on the vehicles were sombre, and surprisingly for ambulances intended for use in 'war scenarios' they did not carry the red cross or medical markings. Most of these vehicles were built to Home Office specifications, although some authorities supplemented their Civil Defence ambulance fleets with former front-line vehicles. A small number of these ambulances still survive, including a Commer model in the care of the Cleveland Ambulance Service.

Top Right:

A standard Home Office specification aluminium body is fitted to this Commer Van ambulance in the Surrey Division, on which the registration number is HPK 109C.

Bottom Right:

This interior view of the same Commer Van shows the storage of stretchers and simple framework for carrying patients. Several vehicles from the Civil Defence fleet saw subsequent service with voluntary organisations such as the British Red Cross, St. John Ambulance and mountain rescue teams. They were also used by a number of Boy Scout troops, and their durable van-like body gave them a good second-hand value for commercial applications.

Above:

It is said that Ford became aware of the potential of the chassis cab market in the early 1960s, when it started to develop its 'V Series Project' that commenced secretly in the autumn of 1961. This series was of course the Transit, which made its public appearance in 1965, but prior to this a lot of work was being done with the Transit's forerunner the Ford Thames. Not least of this preparation was that which was undertaken in connection with ambulances, and Ford's Special Vehicle Department work with the Civil Defence ambulance was to prove invaluable. This Ford Thames van is fitted with a Home Office specification body, and with the registration number 7766 PJ it is pictured in use by the Surrey Division of the Civil Defence.

BEDFORD J1

Another popular ambulance built in large numbers was the Bedford J1 which saw service with many authorities and usually employed bodywork by Herbert Lomas. Bedford had been in the ambulance market for quite a considerable period, and in the post-war era they made significant contributions with both the Utilicon and K1 chassis. Indeed the K-Type continued being sold in significant quantities until the mid-1950s, with ambulance services like Newcastle-upon-Tyne still being loyal to this well-proven model as late as 1956.

Above:
This Bedford J1 of Luton Ambulance Service, registration number UKE 150G, was supplied in 1969. The Luton fleet was incorporated into the Bedfordshire Ambulance Service in the 1974 reorganisation.
Right:
By way of contrast this Bedford J1 has dual-purpose bodywork by Lever constructed for the Joint Oxford City and County Ambulance Service.   Photos: R M Leonard

Top Left:
This Bedford J1 is in the pale blue livery of the Cambridgeshire & Isle of Ely Ambulance Service, and bears the registration number JCE 426F. It has an impressive array of lights at the front, for in addition to the distinctive hooded head lamps and wing-tip sidelights, it also carries blue repeater lights on the grill, a pair of fog lamps, and stalk-mounted indicators on top of the wings.
Photo: R. Leonard

Bottom Left:
As mentioned in the text, the traditional J1 ambulance from Bedford had a long bonnet and separate wings , but this was not always so. Several ambulance services indicated that they wanted an integral body style, and long correspondence was entered into between body builders and Bedford. In 1962 the company agreed to the proposals and both Martin Walter and Lomas produced modern looking ambulances on the TJ1Z. This is a Martin Walter example, but the records do not indicate the authority for which it was built.
Photo. Vauxhall Motors Ltd.

In the early 1950s, Bedford had introduced the A-Type, and with it the basis for the success of the J1 was firmly sown. The reliability of the engine and durability of the chassis provided a great deal of customer satisfaction that would play its part when it came to people ordering J1s. Other special ambulances supplied by Bedford in the 1950s were based on the R-Type lorry chassis, including many for military applications with 4-wheel drive. The S-Type was also used, and a number of articulated tractors were built for ambulance work.

Bus chassis were also used, especially the OB and SB, with examples of the latter type being used extensively by the military. One of the civilian purchasers of this type of ambulance-bus was St. Mary's Hospital at Paddington who took delivery of their SB in 1959. However all this was only the beginning, and as the Bedford TK chassis would help revolutionise the road haulage industry in the early 1960s, the company's TJ chassis would establish a first class reputation for its excellent riding qualities and special suspension.

Commonly known as the J1, this type saw service for many years and proved remarkably reliable and efficient in operation. The J1 generally had a distinctive bonnet and bolt-on wings that featured hooded head lights, however this was not always the case. For example Northamptonshire County Council operated both this type and a more modern looking J1 with a 'squared-off' body that had dispensed with wings. Yet both examples were bodied by Lomas.

Bedford were also at the forefront of technology, and in the early 1960s they began experiments with the firm of Edbro in order to build ambulances with hydraulic tail-lifts. This technological advance enabled wheelchair or stretcher patients to be lifted smoothly in to the back of an ambulance, and certainly eased the strain on ambulance drivers' backs. One of the experimental versions with this tail-lift feature was employed with the City of York Ambulance Service. Along with other advances, ideas such as this helped the J1 maintain its role as a front-line ambulance until well into the early 1970s.

Top Right:
This Bedford J1 with a Lomas body was supplied to the St. John Ambulance on Guernsey, and is photographed in 1971. St. John Ambulance provided ambulance cover on the Island and was known as Guernsey St. John Ambulance (Professional) Service. Its Guernsey registration number was 3575.

Centre and Bottom:
These two views show a good use for an old ambulance, which embodies both practicality and frugality. Here Oxford Ambulance Service have converted one of their Bedford J1s for use as a breakdown and recovery vehicle. The vehicle, registered number TJD 299K was originally a Lever bodied ambulance.
Photo: S Greenaway

THE AUSTIN - MORRIS LD

The introduction of the British Motor Corporation's LD 30cwt forward control van chassis and petrol engine in the 1950s led to several ambulance versions on a proven and economical Austin or Morris base unit. One of the earliest attempts was by the LCC who designed their own body at the Wandsworth workshops. These were originally placed on the standard Austin LD chassis that came complete with a front-end. Technically this was the first use of all plastic (GRP) construction which was soon to be emulated and developed by such companies as Wadhams. After a rigorous testing period, production versions entered service with the LCC in 1959 and these incorporated the use of a cantilevered all plastic front-end assembly unique to the LCC giving a snub 'pig' snout appearance. These vehicles gave long service in London and were known as 'Wandsworth's' to reflect where they had been designed and built.

Left:
The British Motor Corporation (later British Leyland Motor Corporation) LD chassis saw much service throughout the country with bodywork offered by a variety of coachbuilders. One example is this Morris LD from the County of Berkshire Ambulance Service with bodywork by Wadhams and the registration number LMO 22.

Right:
One of the prototype Austin LD ambulances tested by the LCC, its registration number was LLA 232 and the Fleet No. was 'A232'. Note that it still has the original front end fitted.

Below:
A line-up of six Austin LDs that served for many years with the LCC and (after 1965) the GLC when they carried 'London Ambulance Service' lettering. Note the revised front-end treatment and the positioning of the LCC transfer on the crew door. Some of the vehicles have had blue beacons fitted to their roof. The registration numbers in view are, from left to right, 367 BXA, 366 BXA, 365 BXA, 364 BXA and 363 BXA. The fleet numbers would correspond with the number on the registration plate, the first in view is A367.

Above:
Another Morris LD, again with Wadhams bodywork, is pictured in service with the States of Jersey. Bearing its registration number J 1732, the photo was taken in 1971.

Bottom Left:
A preserved example of an Austin with a Wandsworth body, this vehicle (Reg: 394 BXA) is seen in the original 'LCC' livery.
Photo: C Batten

Above:
Several authorities had different types of LD in service at the same time, Huddersfield Corporation for example had Austin, Morris, and BMC badged ambulances in a pale green livery at its new Marsh depot in the 1960s. This photograph shows BMC and Morris badged examples of the LD in service with Reading Ambulance Service carrying registrations PDP 484G and MDP 703F.
Photo: R M Leonard.

Left:
Another preserved example (Reg: ALR 504B) is photographed in the post-1965 'London Ambulance Service' livery with the GLC shield replacing the LCC shield on the side
Photo: M. Newbold

This page:

The larger picture shows a later type Morris LD-5W/Wadhams III ambulance of 1967. It has the registration number KBK 324F, and is pictured in the employ of Hampshire County Council Ambulance Service at the North East Hants Ambulance Station Farnborough).

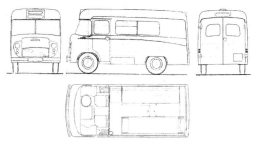

The picture to the right presents the rear view showing the more common double rear doors.

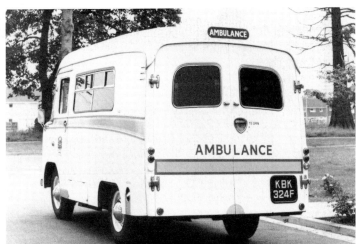

Wadhams further developed the bodywork for the BMC vehicle when it introduced a series III Glass-Reinforced Plastic (GRP) body to fit the LD chassis. Their series III bodywork was constructed from this new material and it made a timely appearance on the ambulance market, heralding considerable publicity when first launched.

The introduction of GRP was to have a great impact on ambulance bodybuilding as it minimised cleaning and maintenance of the vehicle as well as reducing the need for repainting the body. The design achieved with GRP was a complete change from the previous LD bodies, giving the vehicle a streamlined and modern image compared with what had gone before. Numerous authorities purchased it for front line ambulance work after the version first appeared in the early 1960s, and the type proved so popular that it was in continual production until the early 1970s.

There were some slight variations in the bodywork especially the treatment of the front radiator mouldings. London examples for instance, continued the 'Wandsworth' design concept and had a similar snub 'pig' snout front end treatment to enable a bell to be carried.

Top Right:
London as usual adapted the Wadhams bodywork to its own specification with a protruding nose around the front grille on which the warning bell was mounted together with blue flashing repeater lights (registration ALX 786H - Fleet number 'A 1786').
Photos: R M Leonard

Centre:
Most London Wadhams had two rear doors, however a few examples had a single rear door as shown to good effect on this preserved example now maintained by the London Ambulance Service Historic Fleet. (This is PYP 516E, Fleet number 'F 1516 O').

Bottom Right:
Another variety of body applied to the Morris LD and later BMC FG chassis was the Smith-Appleyard 'Statesman' body. This was first introduced in 1959 with a Mark II following in 1962 and a Mark III version in 1966. The 'Statesman' was used by a number of services including the City of Bristol Ambulance Service, Birkenhead Fire & Ambulance Service, Huddersfield and Leeds. The bodies were made of aluminium and the Bristol versions were left in a natural metal state and this earned them the nickname 'Silver Goddess'. This Morris LD/Smith Appleyard 'Statesman' is seen in service with the Avon Health Authority but note the sticker placed over the original City of Bristol crests following re-organisation in 1974.
Photo: R M Leonard.

DENNIS AMBULANCES

Dennis are perhaps more well known for building fire-engines than ambulances, but over the years they have produced some interesting and important ambulance models. In 1956, they launched the Dennis AV series which appeared in several variants from AV1 to AV7. The vehicle was offered as either a 54hp diesel or 78-hp petrol engine versions, with the diesel later being up-rated to 60hp. The original AV1 & 2 was built with a Perkins P4 engine, while the AV3 had a Rolls Royce B40 petrol engine fitted.

The earlier variants had aluminium panelling and the Middlesex Ambulance Service were among the first to place orders when they decided to replace their ageing Morris's that had been in service since the 1940s. The Middlesex Ambulance Service ceased with the 1965 re-organisation, but one of the Middlesex AV2s (5 WMX pictured right) has been preserved as part of the London Ambulance Service Historic Fleet. Many other services operated the various forms of the Dennis AV including Birmingham, Blackpool, Bristol, Coventry, East Ham, Essex, Isle of Wight, Middlesex, Norwich, Rochdale, Southport, Warwickshire and Worcester. In addition, the National Coal Board, British Red Cross Society and St. John Ambulance also operated versions.

Above: *After the NHS Act was introduced in 1948, the service offered by the County Borough of Blackpool was not considered adequate enough and a private company was initially employed. However, 10 years later the council service was fully operational when they took delivery of these five Dennis AVs with Lomas bodies. They are registered MFV 416-420 and allocated the fleet numbers 16 to 20.*
Photo: Derrick A. Andrews
Below: *The preserved Middlesex Ambulance Service AV2, 5 WMX.*
Photo: C. Batten

Left:
Registration number 50 CMX, an AV2 with a split windscreen - note the difference with the picture of the previous Middlesex County Council AV2 from the London Ambulance Service Historic Fleet.
Photo: Chris Batten

*Editor's note: The AV series were extremely well-built, tough vehicles, a fact to which I can personally testify. When a number of the City of Birmingham/Lomas-bodied AV3's were withdrawn in 1968, I was involved in the purchase of three of the class. Two went for service with mountain rescue teams, the other was converted to a mobile caravan. All three saw an interesting and varied life after their official days of service had ended, and two carried on work with an emergency service. Whilst riding in the attendants' seat in the cab of XOL 617, I was involved in a head-on collision with a 20-ton Foden National Coal Board lorry in February 1969 directly outside Doncaster Royal Infirmary. The vehicle was completely written off, but all aboard walked away from the wreckage with barely a scratch. *A.E.*

Another well-known version produced by Dennis was the Karrier-Dennis model from 1962 onwards, which was based on the popular walk-thru chassis cab. Surrey Ambulance Service operated several of these vehicles and they became the main backbone of the county's accident and emergency work replacing the Daimler DC27s which had been in service for well over 10 years. The original batch all had 'Banshee' sirens mounted on the offside front bumper, though later Surrey fitted two-tone horns beneath the roof 'AMBULANCE' sign.

The Surrey vehicles were painted in 'oatmeal cream' with the county service lettering in black on either side of the saloon body. In addition to the emergency ambulance version, Surrey also operated the Karrier-Dennis as a sitting case vehicle. This version also had ramps at the rear to facilitate wheel chair access and clear windows to the saloon.

Inset:
An interior view of the Middlesex AV2, 50 CMX, fleet number 142, showing seating and stretcher arrangements. Note the lack of access to the cab area, due to the fact that the engine cowling was situated between the driver's and attendants' seats.

Left:
A Dennis AV 5/6 of the East Riding of Yorkshire Ambulance Service with the registration number 8123 WF. This variant together with the later AV7 sported a re-styled Dennis PAX frontage as seen on many of the company's Fire Appliances - note the twin headlamps.
Photo: British Ambulance Society Archives via R. Henderson

Top Right:
This Karrier-Dennis from Surrey carries registration number SPD 117F (Fleet No.27) and has the type of two-tone horn mentioned in the text.

Bottom Right:
This contrasting view shows the two types of Karrier-Dennis vehicles employed by the Surrey Ambulance Service. Pictured at their garage the vehicle with the 'L plate' KPC 62C is an emergency unit with a 'Banshee' siren on the front bumper, whilst FPF 706B is a sitting case vehicle with clear windows to the saloon and no blue beacons or siren Photos: R M Leonard.

Above:
*The concept of taking coronary care to the patient is well established today, but one of the pioneers in this field was Professor Frank Partridge from Belfast's Royal Victoria Hospital. He believed that more lives could be saved by the early intervention of trained staff at the scene of a heart attack. In 1966 the Belfast Ambulance Service agreed to provide a Daimler DC27 as a rapid response vehicle, and equipped it with a defibrillator that was about the size of a large suitcase. The power for this came from four large 12v car batteries, which were stowed beneath the fixed central stretcher. The technology may have been in its infancy, but Field's concept was proved true. Accordingly, in 1967 Belfast acquired this (now preserved) Dennis-Karrier (Fleet No. 331) and equipped it as the world's first purpose built Cardiac Ambulance.
Photo: Northern Ireland Ambulance Service.*

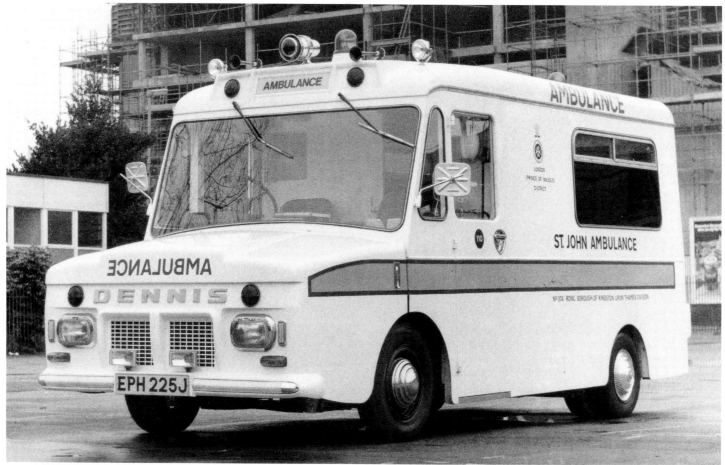

DENNIS FD4

Dennis's next involvement with ambulances was the FD4, which represented an important attempt to produce a truly custom-built ambulance taking into account the views of professionals such as doctors, hospitals and ambulance crews. However, the FD4 story cannot be told without first looking at a design competition held annually up to the 1960s by the SMMT and IBCAM. This was aimed at car and commercial vehicle design, but the 1964 competition unusually included one section for an ambulance based on a chassis drawing supplied by the organisers. The chassis was not named, but was in fact the Dennis Vendor, a somewhat under powered unit first shown in 1960. The winning design was the only one that discarded the Dennis Vendor's ugly front-end style. Four years later, the Dennis FD4 appeared and this had more than a passing resemblance to the 1964-competition winner.

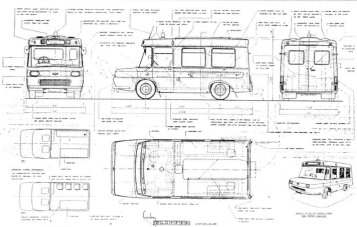

Drawings of 1964 Design Competition Winner; Courtesy of Alan Young

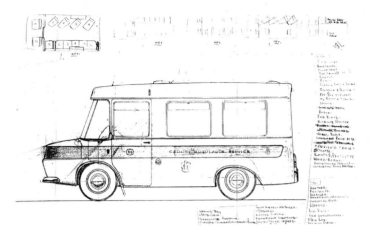

Left:

This picture of the Dennis FD4 in service with the St. John Ambulance Kingston-upon-Thames Division, (registration number EPH 225J) will help show the differences between the two original prototypes; for example, the 1971 version did not have twin body lining. It also had two-tone horns and an American Siro-flashing unit mounted above the roof-box. In this view it will be seen that St. John Ambulance have also fitted front blue repeater flashers either side of the roof box and on the engine cowling.
Photo: R M Leonard

Top Right:
The 1964 Competition, winning entry drawing.

Centre Right:
The first prototype Dennis FD4 on an early test run with no lettering and garage plate 146 P.

Bottom Right:
Front end variation sketches.

The drawings which are presented here show some of the preliminary Design Competition sketches plus a much-reduced copy of the winning drawing. The possible front-end and rear door treatments are innovative. The FD4 had less advanced styling, but clearly Dennis kept the general arrangement of the design competition winner in mind.

The 'Miller Report' sponsored by the Department of Health was another important stage in development, in that it took account of the views of doctors, hospitals and ambulance crews. It was published in two parts, the first recommended having basic standards of training for ambulance personnel, whilst the second dealt with the equipment to be carried by ambulances. Prior to this there was an uncoordinated approach with individual ambulance services deciding their own standard of service and equipment.

As a result of the Miller Report, the National Research Development Corporation (NRDC) sponsored research by a firm of design consultants, Ogle Research, into the feasibility of producing an effective and efficient emergency ambulance with regard to the Miller recommendations. The basic proposals were that the resulting ambulance should be a simple and reliable vehicle, easy to drive and maintain with front-wheel drive to allow a low floor and a petrol engine driven through an automatic transmission. Dennis responded to the challenge and within two years they had produced two prototype front-wheel drive vehicles from the drawing board. This was the Dennis FD4 powered by a Jaguar six-cylinder engine.

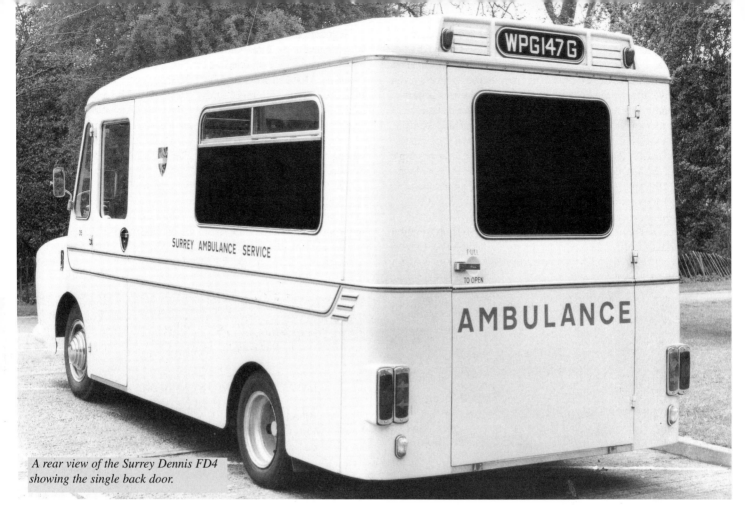

A rear view of the Surrey Dennis FD4 showing the single back door.

The engine originally specified was to be the 2.4 litre petrol unit, but Jaguar then introduced their 2.8 litre engine. As this superseded the 2.4, the more powerful unit was naturally chosen for the FD4 prototypes. The front tyres were larger than those at the rear (Front: 6.00 x 16 radial ply. Rear: 165 x 14 radial ply), and as a result the front tyres had to be changed every 7,000 to 8,000 miles.

The second prototype was displayed at the Commercial Motor Show at Earls Court in 1968, where it carried the livery of Surrey Ambulance Service, whose area covered the Dennis factory at Guildford. Afterwards Surrey allocated it Fleet No.35, whilst they carried out evaluation and tests of this vehicle which bore the registration number WPG 147G.   Dennis retained the first prototype as a test vehicle at their factory, where it created much media interest and was featured on the BBC programme 'Tomorrow's World' as well as in a *Commercial Motor* Road Test (No.12/69).

With such media interest and early signs of success from the first two vehicles, a third example was built and delivered to Rutland Ambulance Service for trials and evaluation. So futuristic was the FD4 that the third vehicle appeared in a sci-fi TV programme minus its Rutland livery. This vehicle differed from the first two in that it had clear body windows rather than the usual dark ambulance glass and the seating arrangements in the saloon were slightly different.

Yet, despite its promising start, problems with the project soon began. Firstly, the Rutland vehicle was written off after an accident with a bus resulted in extensive damage to its front end. Secondly, the interest that had been hoped for from ambulance services did not materialise, and thirdly came the heavy competition from other ambulance chassis makers (who did not seem to be applying the Miller Report). These were the factors that finally led the FD4 project to become stillborn.

Unfortunately for Dennis, by this time Ford had introduced its competitively priced Transit, which with the Bedford CF, quickly proved popular and took over a large percentage of the UK ambulance market. No firm orders for the FD4 came despite the publicity given to the initiative, mainly due to the cost factor, but it was a gallant effort by Dennis to inject new thinking into ambulance design.

Although there were plans to use the first prototype as a works ambulance at the Guildford factory, it was abandoned in a dis-used state in a car park at the works painted in a somewhat strange purple livery. However, an interest was shown in the vehicle by a St. John Ambulance Division (No.374 Royal Borough of Kingston Upon Thames Division) who were still providing agency cover to the London Ambulance Service for accidents and emergencies in the Kingston area at the time. (Actually, the Kingston Division were the last St. John unit to provide such a facility to the London Ambulance Service having originally provided cover for the Surrey Ambulance Service prior to the creation of the GLC in 1965.)

Negotiations were conducted with Dennis and the prototype FD4 was donated to St. John Ambulance after being entirely overhauled and re-sprayed. The vehicle had the registration number EPH 225J (Fleet No.110) and provided front line emergency cover with St. John until the Agency agreement finally ceased in 1975. Later on the Bletchley Division of St. John Ambulance used the vehicle in the Buckinghamshire area. The Surrey service regarded their vehicle as non-standard and it had high costs of spares and maintenance. Finally, having spent most of its operational life at Banstead Ambulance Station, it was sold off at auction. Its fate is not known.

The three FD4s built all had heavy metal bodies, but if it had ever gone into full-scale production the bodies would have been of lighter construction. Although the FD4 would have been welcomed by crews, unfortunately they had little say in the purchasing of vehicles. The Dennis FD4 was estimated to cost about £3,000 at 1968 prices which, although considered reasonable by *Commercial Motor* in their Road Test, was significantly higher than the other alternative chassis.

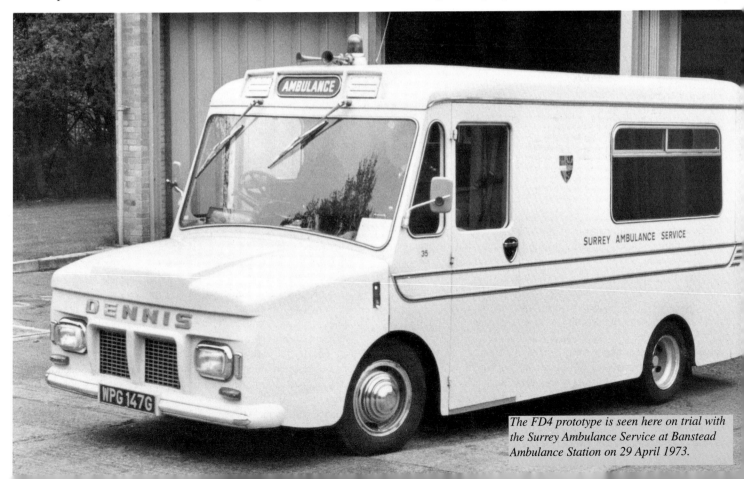

The FD4 prototype is seen here on trial with the Surrey Ambulance Service at Banstead Ambulance Station on 29 April 1973.

THE FORD TRANSIT

Whilst chassis manufacturers (apart from Dennis) seemingly took little notice of the Miller Report, ambulance services did take on board its training and equipment recommendations and these were to impact on future ambulance body design and ambulance operations.

In turn the requirements they began to specify led to a greater improvement in the bodies being placed on the commercially mass-produced chassis cabs offered by people like Ford and Bedford. The opportunity to produce such chassis cabs for a whole variety of applications, and not just specialist use/bodying meant that the price being asked was substantially lower than the bespoke Dennis FD4.

Above:
This petrol engined Transit of Lindsey Ambulance Service is typical of the era, and it bears the registration number YFU 163K.
Right:
Another body variant is this Ford Transit of the Norfolk Ambulance Service, which carries registration number FAH 133K.

Ford chassis had been little used for ambulances during the 1950s and '60s, but not much effort had been put into capturing the important British market. The reasons for this remain unclear, but by the late 1950s Ford had decided to go for the business in a big way. However they did not rush into it straight away, and were seemingly content to court its potential future customers. This may be because its only contender at the time was the Thames van which, whilst being used for Civil Defence ambulance application, was not widely employed in the NHS services.

Yet, with the coming of the Transit (introduced to replace the Ford Thames in 1965) the company suddenly became very pro-active in its marketing of the chassis cab concept. Coupled with the widespread introduction of GRP bodies, the Ford chassis was to become a remarkable innovation. Spurred on by their initial success Ford put significant effort into gaining a foothold in the ambulance market during the early days of the Ford Transit through their Special Vehicle Department, who designed and offered a special 'Ambulance Transit Chassis/Front End'.

Whilst the whole idea of the Transit chassis cab had been simplicity (with a small number of chassis alternatives being capable of meeting a wide range of customer applications), the Special Vehicle Department took note of what ambulance services most wanted. Accordingly they offered a chassis cab with improved suspension to take account of the needs of ambulance work and thus give a superb level of riding comfort. Traditional body builders such as Wadhams and Lomas quickly offered bodies to fit the new chassis and the Transit rapidly established itself as an economical and reliable ambulance. As a result the 'Tranny' was to prove extremely popular for ambulance work and versions were to form the backbone of many services for a number of years, a role the marque still maintains today. Several Transits have been preserved, including WYMAS Fleet No. 400 in West Yorkshire.

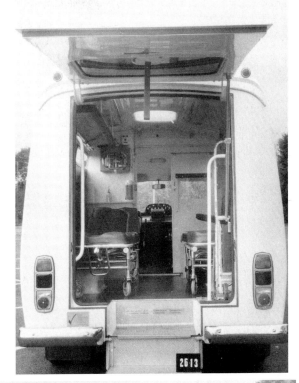

Top Right
A rear view of a City of Lincoln Ambulance Service Transit Custom. In this picture of RVL 726L (taken prior to its entering service) we see the single 'lift-up' tailgate/rear door.

Bottom Right:
This picture of RVL 726L presents a good side view of the bodywork employed. Here we see the styling by Herbert Lomas that so typifies the conventional ambulance of the 1970s. The fact that this style continued into the 1980s and '90s demonstrates its complete suitability for the job at hand.
Photo: M Newbold.

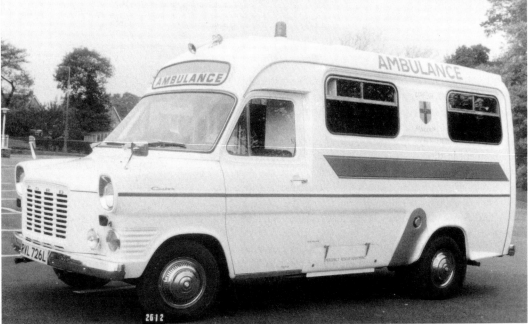

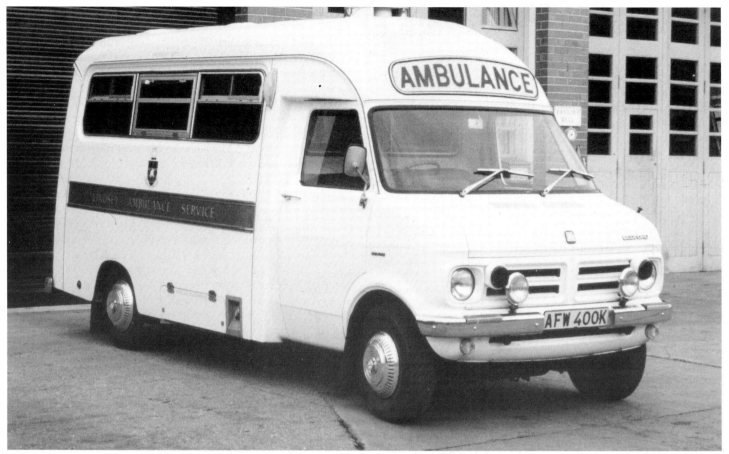

THE BEDFORD CF

The other ambulance chassis that was to make a significant impact around this time was the Bedford CF, which utilised the Bedford 126" wheelbase van chassis of 25cwt nominal payload. Because the dimensions were quite like the Transit's, and the basic requirements of the ambulance services (in light of the Miller Report) were common, the ambulance builders found they could offer very similar bodies on both the Ford and Bedford chassis. However, later in its life the Bedford CF would also be offered in an extended wheelbase version.

This of course capitalised on the success that Bedford had enjoyed with light ambulances in the 1950s and 60s, notably the PCV and the CA van. However, one should not forget that Bedford's associate company, Vauxhall Motors had also been involved in the production of light ambulances for fast emergency and motorway work, and in the early 1960s they had permitted Martin Walter to carry out a number of conversions to the Vauxhall Victor FB as pictured right.

Above: *Vauxhall Victor/Martin Walter Ambulance*: Vauxhall Motors.

This experience proved vital for Bedford as they fought against the might of the Ford marketing campaign. Overall the Transit achieved the greater sales, but Bedford got a fair share of the market. Together, both the Transit and the CF would go on to account for the vast majority of the UK ambulance market for well over a decade, whilst the smaller firms like Dennis failed to make any impression.

Brand loyalty was also becoming a thing of the past, and as one Chief Ambulance Officer recalls, 'By this time they were all beginning to become much of a muchness. And, as overall reliability improved in the chassis being offered, price became a more important consideration.' Some authorities stuck with a single supplier, whilst others (such as Lindsey) operated a mixture of Bedfords and Transits. However, Bedford importantly gained the order to replace the aging London Ambulance Service Wadhams and Wandsworths LDs.

Opposite Page Top:
Lindsey Ambulance Service Bedford CF. Registration number AFW 400K. Lindsey also operated the Ford Transit.
Above:
County Borough of Grimsby Bedford CF registration number CEE 326L. For a number of years a Kingdom Hall of Jehovah's Witnesses was located adjacent to the Grimsby station, but it is said that their church services were regularly punctuated by the sound of two-tone horns. Interestingly the Grimsby fleet originally used to have a sand colour paint scheme, a legacy from the interior coach paint used on the town's bus fleet.
Right:
London Ambulance Service Bedford CF with bodywork by Dormobile, this vehicle OUC 351R is on an extended wheelbase Bedford chassis.

CONCLUSION

This brief look at the first 25 years of the operation of the NHS shows the tremendous change in ambulance development and operation. In 1948, ambulances dating from the 1920s were still in service and crews were very much seen as 'just drivers'.

The co-ordinated provision of ambulance services, initiatives like The Miller Report and technological advances such as the use of GRP, brought about more sophisticated vehicles capable of carrying more life-saving equipment. These were the first steps towards today's advanced paramedic ambulances and their highly trained crews!

The history of the ambulance and the ambulance service has been poorly chronicled over the years, but the **British Ambulance Society** now has the duty of recording and preserving this important part of our motoring and social heritage. It is open to anyone with an interest in anything to do with ambulances from preserving real ambulances to the collection of ambulance uniforms, badges, models and photographs. The longer-term aim is to be able to display all the material within a museum environment. If anyone is interested in joining the Society or has photos such as those shown in this volume that might be borrowed and copied for the archives, they are most welcome to contact the author care of the publishers.

It is hoped that this book will be the first part of a two-volume series covering the 50 years of NHS ambulances between 1948 and 1998. However, if a second volume is to be produced your help and support would be greatly appreciated. If you have enjoyed this book and would like to register your interest in future volumes on British Ambulances please write to:-

The Production Planning Department,
Trans-Pennine Publishing Ltd., PO Box 10, Appleby, CA16 6FA
telephone 01768 351053 or e-mail us at trans.pennine@virgin.net

The End of the Road?
*This view of a St. John Ambulance Bedford J1 in a scrap yard at Hither Green in 1988 illustrates why the **British Ambulance Society** is urgently trying to record ambulance history before it is too late! Can you help with information, memorabilia or photographs such as the inset view of an LCC Bedford K1 taken c1952.*